ONE WEEK

Time

Management
in a week

DECLAN TREACY

Revised by Polly Bird

Hodder Arnold

A MEMBER OF THE HODDER HEADLINE GROUP

Orders: please contact Bookpoint Ltd, 130 Milton Park, Abingdon, Oxon OX14
4SB. Telephone: (44) 01235 827720. Fax: (44) 01235 400454. Lines are open from
9.00–5.00, Monday to Saturday, with a 24 hour message answering service.
You can also order through our website www.hoddereducation.com

British Library Cataloguing in Publication Data
A catalogue record for this title is available from
the British Library

ISBN-10: 0 340 858338
ISBN-13: 9780340858332

First published 1993
Impression number 10 9 8 7 6 5
Year   2007 2006 2007

Copyright © 2002 Declan Treacy and Polly Bird

Typeset by SX Composing DTP, Rayleigh, Essex
Printed in Great Britain for Hodder Education, a division of Hodder
Headline, 338 Euston Road, London NW1 3BH by Cox & Wyman Ltd., Reading.

Hodder Headline's policy is to use papers that are natural, renewable and
recyclable products and made from wood grown in sustainable forests. The
logging and manufacturing processes are expected to conform to the
environmental regulations of the country of origin.

CONTENTS

Preface

Declan Treacy was an inspiration to everyone who wanted to know how to manage their time effectively. As one of the original time management experts he paved the way for a generation of grateful followers. Changes in today's fast moving world mean that this book has had to be updated. Treacy, I'm sure, would have been the first to acknowledge the necessity to keep abreast of the new time management tools and skills available. This new edition is dedicated to his memory.

It's been a hectic day as usual. The phone has rung at least a dozen times, we've attended three meetings, we've spent an hour answering emails, we couldn't begin to count the pieces of paper we've handled, we've dealt with five queries from colleagues who unexpectedly arrived in our office, and there have been two major crises to sort out. We've been so busy but we don't really feel as if we have achieved anything. Even with the wonders of modern technology to help us such as fax machines and mobile phones the work seems to pile up. There seems to be too much to do and just not enough time!

There are 86,400 seconds in each day. Why is it that some people can run large organisations or even countries within that time while others seem to get bogged down in the simplest of jobs? The secret lies in effective time management.

Over the next week we are going to fine tune our time management skills step by step. Each day, we will explore a new topic and after reviewing the theory, the checklists and exercises will encourage us to apply the principles to our own work situation. All the time management techniques recommended in this book are already being practised by successful managers. We only have to look around to see.

Our agenda for the week is as follows:

Sunday	– Self-assessment
Monday	– Mastering paperwork
Tuesday	– Planning
Wednesday	– Controlling IT
Thursday	– Taming the telephone
Friday	– Managing meetings
Saturday	– Managing projects

To get the most out of this book, we will need to set aside one hour a day to work through it. Approximately 45 minutes should be spent reviewing each chapter and completing the exercises, and 15 minutes reviewing our performance at the end of each day. We should start as we mean to go on by blocking off these time periods in our diary now!

For many of its readers, this book will serve as a catalyst for a dramatic change in their working lives; for others, it will serve only to pass a few hours with little real benefit. Only we can determine which category we will fit into. If we choose to change, the benefits of good time management are immediate and substantial. We will:

- Achieve better results
- Improve the quality of our work
- Work faster
- Lower our stress levels
- Make fewer mistakes
- Reduce the number of crises faced
- Increase our salary
- Improve our work satisfaction
- Improve the quality of our non-working life

Remember: *it is what we do during the 86,400 seconds of each day that will ultimately determine how successful we are in our chosen career.*

Involving your colleagues

We need to involve our colleagues in our efforts to manage our time better. As managers we are responsible for the performance of the people around us. If one of our colleagues is buried under a mountain of paperwork the

chaos will have a negative effect upon the rest of the office.
If someone else consistently fails to plan their projects,
everyone else will suffer when the ensuing crisis
materialises. Everyone in our department and throughout
the company should be encouraged to learn how to manage
their time effectively. We should encourage all our
colleagues to read this book. If we demonstrate how
effective its advice is by our own example we will encourage
them to improve their own time management skills. If
possible, we should arrange for a time management expert
to talk to our department and perhaps set aside a day or two
for putting some of the ideas in this book into practice.

We should ask our colleagues to tell us their own ideas for
saving time. It is the people who do the work who
understand the problems. They might come up with ideas
that not only improve their own time management but also
help other people in the department. When everyone in a
department or company becomes involved in improving

their time management skills everyone is motivated to become more productive. If one person slips back into old habits other members of the department can bring them back on to the right track.

Self-assessment

Today, we are going to evaluate our current time management skills. This is a very important exercise and will form the foundation of our future success. By the end of today, we will have completed a time log, made a list of our top 12 timewasters and explored the process by which we will develop timesaving habits.

Self-assessment
- Analysing our current use of time
- Identifying the timewasters
- Changing our habits

Analysing our current use of time

The first step in improving our time management skills is to analyse how we currently spend our time. Research has shown that managers constantly need to change the focus of their attention, and spend an average of only 10 minutes on each task throughout the day. We can easily get swept along in the cut and thrust of daily office life without appreciating where our time goes.

In this section we will complete a self-assessment questionnaire and compile a time log. Both exercises give us the opportunity to stand back and evaluate our performance objectively. A special notebook should be obtained and used for these exercise and all others in the book.

The self-assessment questionnaire:

	Yes	No
I tend not to tackle paperwork the first time I see it	☐	☐
I face more crises than I need to because of poor planning	☐	☐
I sometimes have to be chased by others to get things done	☐	☐
I have a vague idea of what my priorities are	☐	☐
I spend more than 30 minutes a day looking for things	☐	☐
My meetings tend to last longer than necessary	☐	☐
I allow others to negatively influence how I spend my time	☐	☐
I start a lot more projects than I finish	☐	☐
I am always busy but not always productive	☐	☐
I hang on to tasks that should really be delegated	☐	☐

If we have answered 'Yes' to five or more of the statements above then the week ahead will provide us with some much needed insights and solutions to our time management problems. If we have scored less than three on the questionnaire we have probably not been ruthless enough in our self-assessment. Improving our time management skills can only come about through an appreciation of what is currently going wrong. Regardless of our score we should come back to the questionnaire at the end of the week and complete it again.

Compiling a time log will provide us with some additional insights. A time log as shown overleaf should be made up and completed for Thursday and Friday of last week. Each task completed during the day should be written down, along with an estimate of its duration: telephone calls, correspondence, meetings, interruptions, memos, junk mail and so on. We should note down whether the task was planned or not, and then estimate its pay-off. This exercise might also be carried out on Monday and Tuesday of this week to give us a further insight into our time management, and then periodically every few months to gauge our improvement.

Time log

Time	Activity	Pay-off	Duration	Planned
9.00	coffee/chatted with colleagues	low	15 mins	no
9.15	processed mail	med	25 mins	yes
9.40	sales call	low	5 mins	no
9.45	fax arrived	high	20 mins	no
10.05	follow-up call	high	10 mins	no
10.15	colleague dropped by to talk about contract	med	15 mins	no
10.30	sales meeting	med	85 mins	yes
11.55	dealt with telephone messages	med	20 mins	no
12.15	browsed through leaflets left in in-tray	low	10 mins	no
:	:	:	:	:
:	:	:	:	:
:	:	:	:	:
:	:	:	:	:
4.00	draft report for MD	high	70 mins	yes

After completing the time log we should ask ourselves the following questions:

- What proportion of my tasks were planned?
- Was there any real structure to my day?
- Did planned tasks take longer than expected?
- Why did I spend so long on the low pay-off tasks?
- How many interruptions did I face?
- Do I allow others to dictate how I spend my time?
- During what part of the day was I most productive?
- Have I been productive, or just busy?
- What can I do to gain greater control over my time?
- What proportion of my time could I realistically plan for?
- On a scale of 1-10 how would I rate my effectiveness?

Identifying the timewasters

When completing a time log, many people are shocked at the amount of time that is wasted during the day. People we don't need to talk to are on the phone, colleagues are constantly dropping by for a chat, bits of paper are mislaid, meetings last longer than expected. Our days seem to be saturated with timewasters: low pay-off activities that deflect us from the important work .

The list overleaf outlines the 12 most common timewasters. After considering each item on the list we should compile a list of our own top 12 timewasters.

The 12 most common timewasters

1 Losing things
2 Meetings
3 Telephone
4 Interruptions
5 Procrastination
6 Junk paperwork
7 Crises
8 Reverse delegation
9 Perfectionism
10 Distractions
11 Emails
12 Surfing the Internet

Let's look at these timewasters in more detail.

Losing things
How much time is spent rummaging amongst the pile of papers on the desk in the typical week? If we spend just 30 seconds every five minutes extracting an item from the bottom of the in-tray, looking for a telephone number we scribbled down on a loose piece of paper, or locating a misfiled document, it adds up to four hours a week. Time we can't really afford to waste. How often do we have to do things twice because we lost the original?

Meetings
How much of our time is spent in meetings every week? What proportion of that time is wasted due to meetings that should never have been held in the first place? How much time do we waste because meetings start late or overrun?

Do we often have to sit through long meetings and find that only five minutes are relevant to us ?

Telephone

How many times a day are we distracted from important work by the telephone ringing? What proportion of these calls are unexpected? What is the average length of each call? What proportion of these calls are really necessary? Do we allow our calls to drag on for longer than they should? Do we ever find ourselves ringing someone back because there was something we forgot to discuss during the first call?

Interruptions

How many times a day are we interrupted by colleagues arriving at the desk? Are these interruptions really necessary? Does the location of our desk mean that we always catch people's eye as they walk past? Do these interruptions have a negative effect on our performance? Do we encourage social interruptions by always stopping what we are doing and chatting to people?

Procrastination

What tasks have we been avoiding over the past few weeks?
What excuses have been used to delay action? What is
usually the end result of our procrastination?

Junk paperwork

Are we as ruthless as we should be about getting rid of junk
mail or obsolete documents? Do we resist delegating certain
tasks because we enjoy doing them? Do we find ourselves
browsing through magazines, newsletters and brochures
when there is higher pay-off work to be done?

Crises

Do we spend our days spent rushing around dealing with one
crisis after another? Is every crisis we deal with really a crisis?
Is every crisis that we deal with really our problem? If we were
more pro-active would we have avoided some of these crises?

Reverse delegation

Do we respond to requests for help by saying, 'leave it with
me, I'll tackle it later?'. Is there work on the desk that our
subordinates have left for our input?

Perfectionism

Do we spend extra time getting things 100% right when 95% would do? Does our attention to detail on one project mean that something else more important doesn't get done?

Distractions

In the middle of one task, do we often find our attention being grabbed by other work around us on the desk? How do these distractions affect our workflow?

Emails

Do we answer our emails as soon as they arrive? Do we read through all our emails regardless of how many there are and how many are junk and should be deleted unread? Do we print our emails instead of storing them? Do we send emails when a phone call or note would be more appropriate? Do we write long emails when a short one would do?

Surfing the Internet

How many times do we search the Internet for information that could be obtained more quickly and easily by looking in a book or asking somebody? Do we use the Internet as a way of avoiding other work? When surfing the Internet do we get side-tracked by interesting or irrelevant sites?

Working through our own personal list of timewasters, we should ask ourselves how much time we waste in each category during the typical week.

Telephone...	48 mins
Crisis management	45 mins
Meetings	25 mins
Interruptions....................................	19 mins

⋮   ⋮

Surfing the Internet .... 65 mins

Changing our habits

The identification of our timewasters has been a major step
forward. We now need to concentrate on eliminating those timewasting habits and substituting timesaving habits in their place.

Many of these timewasters will have become a natural part
of our work style: allowing meetings to drag on, retaining
junk mail, procrastination. The first time we organised a
meeting that was running over time we probably looked
impatiently at our watch and shuffled our papers but

decided to say nothing. The next time it happened, we might have noted that the meeting was running late, again without commenting. Day after day, week after week, we allowed our meetings to overrun. The timewasting behaviour was repeated so often that it gradually became an unconscious habit. Now our meetings don't finish until everyone has stopped talking. We expect them to drag on and therefore don't even set a finishing time when arranging them.

Now is the time to change; to reverse the process.

Reading this book alone will not help us to alter our timewasting habits; it will take time and effort. If we were learning to play a musical instrument we would not be able to read a book and step straight on to the concert platform to give a virtuoso performance. The psychologists say it takes approximately 21 days to change a work habit. At first, we will have to make a conscious effort to keep our meetings on track and if things are dragging on, we need to stand up and indicate that the meeting is over. It will of course be difficult at first but once we have done it a few times it will become easier. From time to time, we will lapse back into our old habits, but perseverance will bring rewards in the long run. The decision to change is ours alone and the best time to change is now! Twenty years from now, many of this book's readers will be attending seminars and buying books on managing meetings.

The four-step process of change
The four-step process below should be applied to each of our timewasters. Procrastination will be used as an example.

If procrastination is one of our major timewasters, we probably put off things using excuses such as, 'I'm too busy right now', 'I need to wait for more information', or 'I'll do it tomorrow'. We might start off at the beginning of the day by pushing aside just one item, but it is soon joined by other documents. As more and more unfinished papers join the pile at the bottom of the action tray, we resist approaching that part of the desk. If we tackle one item, we will have to face everything, causing an immediate flood of guilt and stress. Subconsciously, we say to ourselves, 'Now what can I do instead ?'.

1 Write down the timewaster
On the top of a new page in our time management notebook we should write down the timewaster we wish to tackle: Procrastination.

2 List the problems caused by the timewasting habit
Next we need to list the problems faced as a result of procrastination: constantly feeling guilty about unfinished work, increased stress levels, spending too much time on the enjoyable things which bring few rewards, a reputation around the office as someone who is unreliable.

3 Visualise the timesaving habit
All thoughts of procrastination should be removed from our minds and we should visualise ourselves as 'doers'. What would things be like in the office if we had the reputation for getting things done, rather than for procrastinating? How would we handle our correspondence? How would we approach difficult reports? How much unfinished work would there be lying in the in-tray? The benefits of being a 'doer' should be written down.

4 Develop the timesaving habit
Next we need to write down the steps that are necessary to change our timewasting habit:

a I will stop using phoney excuses like, 'I need to wait for more information';

b I will have to remove tempting distractions such as brochures and magazines from my line of sight;

c I need to spend more time planning my day;

d I need to break down large projects into more manageable tasks;

e I will finish the uncomfortable items first and then reward myself with more enjoyable tasks.

This four-step process should be followed for each of our top 12 timewasters. One page in our time management notebook should be devoted to each timewaster: listing the problems it causes, visualising the way we want things to be in future and writing down the steps we need to take to change our timewaster to a timesaver. Every day during the the coming week, a few minutes should be spent reviewing our notebook to remind ourselves of the things that need to change.

Adapt to suit the environment

No matter how effectively we plan, we must always be prepared to adapt to changing circumstances. Often we can predict likely changes in advance. If we get a lot of phone calls in the morning, we should not schedule an urgent task for that time. If our boss delegates work late in the day, we should try to get our 'A' priority work done before then so that we are not swamped with work. If we face a lot of genuine crises, then we should only plan a small proportion of the day.

The KISS principle

The KISS (Keep It Short and Simple) principle should be applied to everything we do. It is a waste of time holding a meeting if the matter can be resolved by a quick phone call. There is little value in writing a 10-page report where two pages are all that is necessary. There is no need to send a memo to someone when we bump into them several times a day. Introducing a form is unnecessary if the information asked for can be obtained elsewhere. We should go back and look at the time logs we completed on Sunday and ask ourselves which activities would not have been undertaken if the KISS principle was used.

Adopt a positive outlook on life

A positive outlook on life can only increase our chances of being successful. Excuses can always be found for the problems that confront us. With a negative outlook we spend our time complaining and blaming others for our problems instead of working to find a solution. Of course, it is not always easy to be positive, but in the long term we will be rewarded. A positive outlook will also motivate the people around us to get things done. Looking back over the past week, we should mentally list all the time management problems that we blamed on others, rather than asking what we could do to eliminate them.

Perfectionism can be dangerous
In some cases, it is wise to pay attention to detail but in many cases it can be counterproductive. To get something 90% right will often suffice. If we spend time getting internal memos, reports, presentations or projects 100% right it often means that something more important is left in the in-tray. Furthermore, the extra time we spend on any one task is rarely worth the extra pay-off. The law of diminishing returns comes into play. If we are preparing something for someone else, we should agree on a level of performance that is acceptable. There is absolutely no benefit to the company if we spend an extra 30 minutes printing an internal report again to correct a few spelling mistakes. If others are drafting letters or reports for us, we should try to avoid editing their work. We have to appreciate that others may say things in a slightly different way to us, but which is no less valid.

Tomorrow, we will focus on conquering the paper mountain. We cannot begin to manage our time effectively until we have gained control of the paper flow.

Mastering paperwork

Despite predictions about the move towards the paperless office, we still seem to be drowning in a sea of paper, much of it unnecessary. Today, we are going to look at ways of controlling the constant flow of paperwork arriving on the desk. By the end of the day, the desk will be clear of paperwork, we will have implemented techniques for reducing the inflow of unnecessary paperwork, and we will have streamlined and reorganised our files. This is necessary because it is essential to create the right physical environment before we can begin to manage our time effectively.

Mastering paperwork

- Paperwork reduction campaign
- Effective paper handling
- Effective filing

Paperwork reduction campaign

Low pay-off paperwork is costly to generate and it deflects attention away from what is important. If we examine all the memos, reports, faxes, letters, magazines, invoices, junk mail and other bits of paper that arrive on a daily basis, it becomes clear that most of it should never have been generated in the first place.

We frequently blame others for our paperwork problems, but it is often our own work style that causes the heavy inflow of paper. How often can we be heard to say to

colleagues, 'Send me a copy for my files', 'Could you confirm that in writing?', 'Write me a report on it', 'Send a memo around to everyone', or 'I can't act on that unless I have it in writing'? Before asking others to send paperwork, we should ask ourselves if the information is really necessary. If we need the information, we should try to obtain it by word of mouth or through the computer. Paper should be our last resort. We also complain about the amount of junk mail we receive but then deal with unwanted telesales callers by saying, 'Send me some information'.

And what about the paper that we create and keep? Do we really need to print a hard copy of each email we send and receive or every computer file we create? They all add to the piles of paper on our desk or clutter up our files. We can surely delete most of them or store them on our computer.

As well as reducing the inflow of paperwork, we need to cut down the outflow from the desk. If we are constantly distributing forms, memos and photocopies to others, we can expect nothing less than an avalanche of paperwork in return. We should spend 30 minutes today devising and implementing strategies for reducing paperwork. The checklist below serves as a useful starting point.

Paperwork reduction checklist

- Have name removed from external mailing lists
- Remove name from internal circulation lists
- Ask colleagues to be concise
- Where necessary have paperwork rerouted
- Talk to people instead of writing
- Ask colleagues to report by exception
- Reduce the volume of paperwork leaving the desk
- Return unnecessary paperwork to sender

We should set a definite target for reducing paper in the office over the next few months and enlist the help of our colleagues. Less paper means lower costs, improved productivity, improved morale, improved communications and a better service for our customers.

Effective paper handling

Ideally, each piece of paper that arrives on the desk should be handled only once. Few of us can afford the luxury of picking up the same piece of paper again and again without actioning it. If we are handling the same bits of paper over and over again we will be extremely busy but at the end of the day we will not have actually achieved anything extra.

The measles test

An exercise that will encourage us to handle paperwork the first time we see it is the measles test. For the next week, every time we pick up a piece of paper to deal with it, we should use a red marker and place a red dot on the page. If by the end of the week most of the paperwork on the desk has had an outbreak of measles, then we know we need to change our habits.

The lack of a system for processing incoming paperwork, combined with our natural tendency to be indecisive, results in stacks of unfinished paperwork building up on the desk. Many of us work in chaotic environments and rationalise it with statements such as, 'I know where everything is!', 'It suits my personality!' or 'It's organised chaos!'.

We can always find an excuse, but research and common sense tells us that the chaotic desk leads to:

- Low productivity
- Missed opportunities and deadlines
- Frantic searches for lost information

- Long working hours
- High stress levels
- Low morale
- Unwanted distractions
- Unexpected crises

If we think back over the past week we will have experienced many of the problems on the list because of our desktop chaos.

Before we can begin to process the flow of paperwork efficiently, we need to clear the desk. The clear-out should start today, with all the junk we have accumulated on the desk: glossy brochures, obsolete reports, magazines we will never read, memos we will never look at again. These items will have accumulated because they looked interesting at first glance and we put them aside telling ourselves we would look at them again when we had more time .

Once the desk has been cleared, it should remain clear. Many people say, 'I know I have lots of paper on the desk but it's only junk it's not real work!'. This junk however hides the important paperwork; it constantly distracts us and when we are procrastinating about an item of real work, this junk becomes infinitely more attractive and worthwhile. Operating a clear-desk policy does not mean that we will never be seen with paperwork on the desk again. It means that we should restrict our workspace to one project at a time. We should also try to avoid having a clear desk whilst having every other available space in the office piled high with paper.

The RAFT technique

The RAFT technique should be used to keep us afloat on the sea of paperwork. As soon as a piece of paper arrives we should make a definite decision about what to do with it and move on. There are in fact only four things we can do with a piece of paper that lands on the desk: **R**efer it, **A**ct on it, **F**ile it or **T**hrow it away.

Our referred paperwork should go straight in the out-tray, filing paperwork belongs in the filing system, junk should go straight in the bin and, where possible, our action paperwork should be dealt with straight away. Any "act on" paperwork not dealt with immediately should go in a bring-forward file. We should have a place for everything and everything should go in its place.

Paperwork management checklist

- Be decisive when dealing with incoming paperwork
- Try to handle each piece of paper only once
- Avoid using a plethora of diaries and notepads
- Restrict the workspace to one project at a time
- Try to avoid high-rise trays on the desk
- Avoid using the in-tray as a storage space
- Use the RAFT technique
- Set up a bring-forward file for tracking unfinished paperwork
- Sort out the papers in our briefcase every day

Effective filing

The filing system, whether paper or electronic, is one of the most important management tools we have. We will concentrate on our paper files today, but the same general principles should be applied to computer files.

Unfortunately, filing is often seen as a clerical activity and not worthy of management attention. As a result, our filing systems tend to be poorly organised. Stacks of 'to file' paper build up on the desk, increasing the chances of items being mislaid. When we do file paperwork, it tends to be done in a haphazard fashion with the focus on getting the documents out of sight. We rarely give any thought to the question of finding them again.

To win back control of our filing system, we are first going to look at overcoming our tendency to hoard too much information. Then we will reorganise our files to make things easier to find.

De-junking the filing system
If we take a brief look through our files, we will probably find that most of their contents are obsolete: abandoned projects, glossy brochures, out-of-date reports, untouched reading material. In fact, studies have shown that approximately 85% of the information we keep will never be looked at again and 45% are already stored somewhere else.

We should try to set aside 90 minutes today for purging our files. Working through the folders one by one we should consign to the bin all those items that:

a we will never get the time to look at;
b can easily be located elsewhere if needed;
c have a low pay-off attached to them.

If we are sufficiently ruthless, then the contents of our filing systems should be reduced by more than 50%. One rule that is adopted in many bureaucratic organisations is, 'Before throwing anything out, make a copy of it just in case you might need it again'. The rule should be taken with a pinch of salt, but it identifies the fear that many people have when throwing things away. We tell ourselves that someone is bound to need the document at some time in the future. If we talk to people who are ruthless about binning things, they

will say that junked items are very rarely needed again and when that happens there is always a copy somewhere else.

Once the clear-out is complete, we should try to keep the quantity of files down by:

- Purging our files as we use them on a daily basis
- Asking others to retain copies of documents they send us
- Marking items with a discard date
- Never keeping copies of the same document in different files
- Asking others to keep paperwork concise
- Transferring infrequently-used files to archives

Reorganising the files

The better organised our files, the more likely we are to make use of the information we keep. There is an important filing maxim which states, 'If you don't know you have it, or you can't find it, then it's of absolutely no use to you'.

Very few of us have ever sat down and considered setting up a logical filing system. Our file headings are usually created with little thought and file folders are usually arranged at random in the drawer. We only have to watch ourselves and others trying to retrieve mislaid items from the filing cabinet to realise the importance of a good classification system.

There are six main ways of classifying information:

- By subject category
- Alphabetically
- By date
- By colour
- Geographically
- Numerically

We should experiment with different combinations of the above classifications until we develop a system that suits our way of working. Once we have decided on a suitable system, we will need physically to reorganise the files. The file management checklist below will help us in that endeavour.

File management checklist

- Use simple file headings
- Subdivide bulging folders
- Separate active files from infrequently-used records
- Put the filing cabinet within reach of the desk
- Don't allow stacks of filing to build up on the desk
- Use a classification system that can be trusted
- Purge files regularly

Filing on computers

Now that computers have become standard office machines we can use them to our advantage to keep our emails and computer document files under control. The techniques are similar to filing paper. We need to decide which files to delete, which to pass on and which to keep so that we can easily retrieve the ones we need to work with. Before we save any computer file we must decide whether it can be safely deleted or whether it should be saved. If the file should be saved the next question is where to file it.

Sorting into folders

Word processing documents, spreadsheets, emails and other computer files can all be sorted into folders and sub-folders. The computer manual and on-line help will show how your applications save files. Choose obvious names for your main folders such as Project A, Staff or Book. Then subdivide these into relevant folders. So, for example, we could divide the Project A folder into folders for project outline, control and folders for the input of individual staff members Tom's Section. Or the folder for the best selling book we are writing in our lunch break could be divided into folders for each chapter, the outline, character descriptions and letters from publishers. We can then move each computer document into the relevant sub-folder. We can also scan paper documents into our computer and save them in the relevant folders.

Setting up filtering systems
Incoming emails can be filtered into relevant folders. Our email help box will tell us how to do this. For example, we can filter all emails with $ or £ signs or the word 'win' in the subject line to a folder marked 'junk'. We can then periodically delete this folder without reading the contents. We can also filter emails from particular people or groups into separate folders. So all emails from our boss can be filtered into one folder and dealt with first.

Once we have our paperwork under control, we free up our time for more productive pursuits.

Tomorrow we shall concentrate on planning.

Planning

Today, we will look at planning on three levels. We will start off by looking into the future to set long-term business and personal goals. Next we will devise the action plans which provide the blueprint for turning our dreams into reality. Finally we will look at planning on a daily basis.

> *Planning*
>
> • Setting goals
> • Devising action plans
> • Daily plans

Planning is one of the most important time management skills. Our goals give us a sense of direction in both our personal and business lives. Those people who lack a clear vision of where they are going, spend a large proportion of their time reacting to the demands of others: urgent faxes, emergency telephone calls, asap memos and crisis meetings. No matter how efficient we are in dealing with those short-term demands it is difficult to be successful in the long term without plans. Accidental success is quite rare.

Setting goals

Successful companies have goals: to achieve the highest market share, for instance or to have the most efficient production line. Without these goals things would be chaotic. Successful athletes have goals: to break the world record, or to win a gold medal at the Olympics. Athletes would not get up to train at 5 a.m. on a cold winter's morning unless they had a clear vision of standing on the podium receiving a trophy. Successful managers also have clear goals.

Creative visualisation
Half an hour should be set aside today for an exercise in creative visualisation. We are going to sit back and dream of the future, banishing all negative thoughts from our minds. It is easy to be self-critical and to tell ourselves, 'I could never achieve that'. Long-term goals, such as running our own business, initially appear to be beyond our reach. In the next section we will look at breaking down our goals into manageable action plans. Once we have completed an action plan, all we have to do is concentrate on one step at a time. Before starting the creative visualisation process, we should ensure that we won't be disturbed.

Our look into the future should focus on both our work and our family lives. We should try to see ourselves in one, five, 10, 15 and 20 years from now. The questions overleaf will help us in that process.

Business goals

- What would I like to have achieved by the time I retire?
- What salary would I like to earn?
- Would I like to run my own business or become a senior manager in a large organisation?
- Should I remain in this country or work abroad?
- Would I benefit from further education?
- What business skills do I need to develop?
- What industry would I really like to work in?
- What is my ideal job?
- What professional organisations should I join?

Once we have visualised a successful future in our working lives we need to consider our personal lives and aim to achieve a healthly balance between the two.

Personal goals

- What hobbies/special interests would I like to pursue?
- Where would I like to live?
- Do I need to spend more time with the family?
- What parts of the world would I like to see?
- Should I learn a new language?
- Do I need to adopt a healthier diet?
- Could I improve my level of fitness?
- What sort of home would I like to live in?

As we visualise our future achievements we should write them down as goals in our time management notebook.

We should hold a creative visualisation session every six months because certain goals may have been reached or, due to circumstances beyond our control, certain goals may have changed slightly. Each time we achieve a goal, we should set another one so that we are always working towards a more fulfilling business and personal life.

Devising action plans

Unless we make definite plans we cannot hope to turn our dreams into reality. The action plans we devise for each of our goals will provide step-by-step guidelines for achieving those goals.

The benefits of action plans are clear to all those who use them.

Action plans:

- Break down daunting goals into achievable steps
- Motivate us to achieve our goals
- Make implementation of ideas easier
- Provide us with a useful overview
- Enable us to focus on the important rather than the urgent
- Provide a benchmark against which we can judge progress
- Help us to anticipate problems

The steps we need to take to achieve each of our goals should be written down on the relevant page in our time management notebook. If we have a goal to be MD of a large company we should work back from the goal and ask ourselves, 'What do I need to do to get there?'. Any major steps we need to take should be broken down into smaller more achievable steps. We should also set a deadline for achieving our goal and deadlines for achieving each step along the way.

An important question we need to ask ourselves is, 'What will it cost to achieve the goal?'. There may be a substantial financial cost involved, such as investing in an MBA programme. There may also be a personal cost involved. If we are going to set up our own business, it may mean we have less time to spend with family and friends. So, we need to weigh up the cost of achieving our goals against their pay-off.

Daily plans

Once our action plans are complete, we need to shorten the time frame and look at compiling daily plans or 'to-do' lists.

Daily plans:

- Enable us to plan our work sensibly
- Act as reminders
- Unclutter the mind
- Help us to keep track of deadlines
- Motivate us to get things done
- Help us to focus on priorities

Eight steps to effective daily plans
We are now going to look at a straightforward process for compiling daily plans. The medium on which we capture our plans is not as important as the process. Electronic to-do lists, index card systems, personal organisers, or desk diaries can all be used effectively.

1 Five minute planning period

At the end of each day we should spend five minutes planning the next day. As we turn the page of our diary there should already be a number of things to do, commitments and action plan steps which have been carried forward from previous days. For example:

To do	Priority	Completed	Delegate	Time
Call John				
Finish marketing report				
Read article				
Arrange meeting with M.G.				

2 Carry forward today's unfinished activities

If there are any activities on today's to-do list they should be carried forward to tomorrow or another suitable date. If we frequently find ourselves with a large number of unfinished tasks at the end of the day, we are probably trying to squeeze too much into the day. We should therefore leave more room in the day for unplanned events.

To do	Priority	Completed	Delegate	Time
Call John				
Finish marketing report				
Read article				
Arrange meeting with M.G.				

To do	Priority	Completed	Delegate	Time
Call T.D.				
Reply to B.C.G letter				
Finalise budgets				
Send file to A.C.				

3 Plan tomorrow's activities

Taking account of our scheduled activities such as meetings and appointments, list the activities to tackle tomorrow.

To do	Priority	Completed	Delegate	Time
Call John				
Finish marketing report				
Read article				
Arrange meeting with M.G.				
Call T.D.				
Reply to B.C.G letter				
Finalise budgets				
Send file to A.C.				
Copy for brochure				
Check travel arrangements				
Send slides to bureau				
Prepare mailshot				
Read next chapter of this book				

4 Include goal-related activities
We should always include activities that will help us to
achieve our long-term goals. When busy we tend to react to
the urgent items rather than the items that will benefit us in
the long run. It is important therefore to always include goal
related activities on our to-do list.

To do	Priority	Completed	Delegate	Time
Call John				
Finish marketing report				
Read article				
Arrange meeting with M.G.				
Call T.D.				
Reply to B.C.G letter				
Finalise budgets				
Send file to A.C.				
Copy for brochure				
Check travel arrangements				
Send slides to bureau				
Prepare mailshot				
Read next chapter of this book				
Co. MBA sponsorship?				
Buy French tapes				

5 Prioritise things to do
Working through the list, we should prioritise each activity.
Our goal-related activities should always be assigned an 'A'

priority; items with associated deadlines are the same, as are items with high pay-offs. 'B' priorities will include those items we would like to get done but which can be delayed if we don't have the time. Anything we think should be assigned a 'C' priority should be crossed off the list – we have better things to do with our time.

To do	Priority	Completed	Delegate	Time
Call John	B			
Finish marketing report	B			
Read article	B			
Arrange meeting with M.G.	A			
Call T.D.	B			
Reply to B.C.G letter	B			
Finalise budgets	A			
Send file to A.C.	B			
Copy for brochure	A			
Check travel arrangements	B			
Send slides to bureau	A			
Prepare mailshot	B			
Read next chapter of this book	A			
Co. MBA sponsorship ?	A			
Buy French tapes	A			

6 Delegate activities

No manager should ever get bogged down in a mountain of paperwork because it can always be delegated. Working through our to-do list we should ask ourselves who the best person is to deal with each item. In delegating, we should be seeking to develop the skills of the people around us rather than dumping work on them.

To do	Priority	Completed	Delegate	Time
Call John	B			
Finish marketing report	B		J.D.	
Read article	B			
Arrange meeting with M.G.	A			
Call T.D.	B			
Reply to B.C.G letter	B			
Finalise budgets	A		J.D.	
Send file to A.C.	B			
Copy for brochure	A			
Check travel arrangements	B		A.H.	
Send slides to bureau	A			
Prepare mailshot	B			
Read next chapter of this book	A			
Co. MBA sponsorship?	A			
Buy French tapes	A			

7 Estimate the length of time each task requires
This process is difficult until we get used to it. When we
have totalled up our estimates along with our scheduled
activities they should not add up to more than 75% of the
working day. It is important not to try to plan every minute;
we need to be flexible in order to accommodate the
unexpected.

To do	Priority	Completed	Delegate	Time
Call John	B			10
Finish marketing report	B		J.D.	60
Read article	B			15
Arrange meeting with M.G.	A			5
Call T.D.	B			10
Reply to B.C.G letter	B			20
Finalise budgets	A		J.D.	5
Send file to A.C.	B			5
Copy for brochure	A			30
Check travel arrangements	B		A.H.	5
Send slides to bureau	A			10
Prepare mailshot	B			20
Read next chapter of this book	A			60
Co. MBA sponsorship?	A			10
Buy French tapes	A			5

8 Work through mail and make additions to list
Tomorrow morning our mail will invariably throw up a
number of important things to do. These should be added to
our list.

To do	Priority	Completed	Delegate	Time
Call John	B			10
Finish marketing report	B		J.D.	60
Read article	B			15
Arrange meeting with M.G.	A			5
Call T.D.	B			10
Reply to B.C.G letter	B			20
Finalise budgets	A		J.D.	5
Send file to A.C.	B			5
Copy for brochure	A			30
Check travel arrangements	B		A.H.	5
Send slides to bureau	A			10
Prepare mailshot	B			20
Read next chapter of this book	A			60
Co. MBA sponsorship?	A			10
Buy French tapes	A			5
Check invoice	*B*			*10*
Discuss complaint with sales	*A*			*20*
				$\overline{295}$

Once tomorrow's to-do list is complete we are ready to attack the day. The temptation is often to start on the quick and easy activities, ticking off many items on the list. The only effective way to work however, is to tackle our activities in order of priority. As a general rule, we should not tackle a B priority item unless all our A priorities have been completed. It can be useful to set aside a 'quiet hour' in the day when we know we will not be disturbed for tackling important items. Where possible, similar activities should be grouped together: telephone calls, correspondence, or delegation to secretary.

The realities of prioritising

In an ideal world we would move from one task to another in the order we prioritised them. Unfortunately, life isn't like that. Just because we have prioritised actions does not mean that we can always complete them in order. New instructions from our boss or the problems associated with dealing with crises mean that priorities get changed. The importance of prioritising our daily plan is that it keeps us focused when we need to get back on track. Once we have dealt with the immediate demands from our boss or solved a crisis we can see from our plan immediately what other work we need to do and which work should be completed first. We may never get to the end of our daily list but we can be reasonably sure that we are dealing with our most important work.

The manager's emergency prioritising trick:

Take all your papers and quickly sort them into three piles:

- now
- later
- unimportant

Take the first pile only and quickly sort it according to the order in which tasks must be done that day. Concentrate only on that pile and work through it steadily, starting with the task you have prioritised as the most important.

Time and travel

Executives are spending more and more of their time travelling, both nationally and internationally. The time spent travelling can eat into our productive working time. Careful preparation before major trips is essential. Some time should be spent writing down a list of objectives for the trip and then collecting together all the necessary paperwork. We should keep a travel file for collecting together all our travel documents, and prepare a special file containing the background information for meetings we will be attending. During the trip, it is essential to keep all our papers under control, because the chaos is very difficult to unravel when we get back to the office. At the end of each day, we should review our paperwork for the day, try to deal with any action points on the spot, and discard any unnecessary documents.

On long or short trips, we can always make use of our travel time. It is an ideal opportunity to catch up on our reading. Magazines, newsletters, reports, routine correspondence should be collected in a reading file so that we can catch up when travelling. If we find it difficult to read while travelling, we can substitute the spoken word; most of the business bestsellers are now available in audio format. As portable computers become more widely available, we can use our travel time even more productively, catching up on correspondence or writing reports.

Using computers for planning

Computers and electronic organisers are now common planning tools. Used effectively they can make planning easier and save time. Many organisers can be connected to a desk top computer. This means we need not write out our diaries or plans more than once. We can record details away from the office on our laptop or organiser and then later transfer them to our desk top machine.

Co-ordinating diaries

Whether we use a paper diary or an electronic organiser we need to ensure that we co-ordinate them with our secretary's diary or whoever else needs to be informed. This should be done at least at the beginning and end of each day.

The pay-off from our long-term plans is never immediate and that is why many people adopt a reactive approach to time management. Urgent and immediate tasks will always give us an instant pay-off whereas a longer term, pro-active approach will delay the pay-off but it will always be much greater. A useful principle to bear in mind when working through our to-do list is the 80:20 rule: 80% of our results come from 20% of our activities. Thus 80% of our sales come from 20% of our customers, 80% of our achievements will come from 20% of our paperwork and conversely 20% of that report we have to read will give us 80% of the information we need.

Tomorrow, we will look at controlling IT.

Controlling IT

The Information Technology (IT) we use is faster and more powerful than ever before and the use of computers is widespread and vital in today's modern business world. This should mean that we become more productive and work more efficiently. However, it can also encourage us to waste time unless we use it effectively. Today we will look at the technology we use and discover how to get the best use from it.

Getting the most from computers

The computer is undoubtedly the main office took of today. Used effectively it can be a powerful means of communication and an effective planning tool. Modern computer applications and powerful computers mean that they can make time management quicker and easier. But they are only as effective as the software they use and the people who use them. No matter how large and expensive a computer might be, unless the person using it knows how to get the most out of it, it might remain an expensive office toy. Computer planning applications include on-screen organisers, diaries, calendars and forms and these, as well as the standard office applications, can make time management easier.

A computer can also be an efficient way of gathering information when connected to the web through the Internet. Office computers are often connected to an intranet which is a kind of private Internet restricted to users within one company. It enables communication between individuals and departments in a company. It is easy to confuse the Internet and intranet.

The difference between the Internet, the web and intranet:

Internet
- The worldwide physical networks of computers that communicate using common protocols

The web
- The content of the Internet consisting of many pages on different sites usually containing text and graphics

Intranet
- A self-contained Internet with a website that can only be used within an internal company network.

Using the intranet

The company intranet is largely a library of information that is accessible to all staff. Because it is designed for internal use only we may need a password to access it. We should not assume that everyone will see everything we post on the intranet. It may be necessary to use a brief email to alert staff to any new information posted. On the other hand we should be careful what we post on our intranet because everyone in the company could read it.

Do not use the intranet to:

- Post personal information for everyone to see
- Write long rambling pieces
- Post personal remarks about other staff
- Give information that should be presented in person or in a personal memo.

Using the Internet

The Internet is a world-wide source of information but it can be frustrating and time-wasting if we don't know how to use it. We should remember that basic information is often quicker and easier to obtain from a book, a phone call or a question to colleague. Information on the Internet and the web can be posted by anyone so when we find a page that looks useful we need to check the source and see if it mentions when the pages were last updated to judge whether it is reliable. A recently updated page posted by a government agency, for example, is likely to be more reliable than one several years old posted by an individual. Each website has a unique web address known as an URL (Uniform Resource Locator). When we find a reliable and useful website we should make sure we can reach it again by saving it in our favourites list on our computer. To save time when searching for information we should make our request as specific as possible.

Online time-saving tips

Going online whether to the Internet or an intranet can be addictive. A great deal of time is wasted by people who play games online, transact personal business or spend hours 'surfing the net' unnecessarily. We must not use the web as an excuse for not getting on with other work. The Internet should not be accessed during office hours without the employers' permission. Some companies severely restrict employees' use of the Internet as opposed to the company intranet. Using the Internet for personal business or playing games is usually forbidden.

Save time when online by:

1   Restricting your searches to specific pieces of information.

2   Making your search request as specific as possible.

3   Only going online for information that cannot be obtained more quickly and easily from traditional sources – or by asking a colleague.

4   Asking your secretary or administrative support person to make searches for you.

5   Setting a personal time limit for searches – e.g. ten minutes maximum.

6   Make a list of information you need and search for them in order allowing three attempts only for each question.

Other timesaving machines

There are many other useful machines that help to make our work easier and save us time. By eliminating paper and enabling us to work wherever we are they reduce the amount of time we have to spend on filing or hunting for information.

Laptop computers
Although a desk top computer is standard office machinery some companies provide their staff with laptops or employees may have laptop computers of their own. Laptop computers can often be connected to a desk top machine via a port or infra red connection. This makes it easy to transfer work done away from the office. We should not be like the business people who use laptops on trains and who are more often than not playing solitaire or patience on them. Keep game playing for weekends.

Advantages and disadvantages of laptop computers:

For
- Easy to transport out of the office
- Can be used to work at home
- Can be connected to a desk top computer
- Can be used to give off-site presentations

Against
- More vulnerable to theft
- Can be heavy to carry

Laptop computers can be useful for giving off-site presentations. The presentation can be prepared in the office using a graphics program and transferred to a laptop either directly or by disk. The laptop can then be carried to the presentation site and be used to give a presentation on the spot. Laptops may have batteries that only last for a couple of hours so a mains lead should be kept with it and used whenever possible.

Electronic organiser PDAs
Electronic organisers or PDAs (Personal Digital Assistants) store contact details and notes and some have word processing or spreadsheet programs. They are small enough to fit into a briefcase, handbag or pocket and can be used to keep contact details to hand. The versions of word processing and spreadsheet programs installed may be scaled down versions of the main applications. Some PDAs can be connected to mobile phones for email and Internet use. Make the best use of them by:

- using short cut keys for frequently used numbers
- using a PDA that has the same applications as your desk top computer
- keep personal and work contacts in separate files

Scanners
Scanners save time by reducing paperwork because scanned documents, business cards, invoices etc. can be stored on a computer. Scanned documents can be sent straight from a computer by fax or as an email attachment. The original document can be destroyed once it has been scanned into a computer.

Fax

Faxes can be sent from stand alone fax machines or straight from a computer either as scanned documents or written directly into the computer's fax template. Faxes are particularly useful for image based documents or those with a signature. Have a standard cover sheet prepared with your own and your company contact details clearly printed on it.

Getting the most from the software

Computers usually come with standard applications such as spreadsheet, word processing programs, a graphics package, a database and an organiser. We often underuse these programs because we don't know their full capabilities and only learn how to use them by trial and error. We should ensure that we ask for training in how to use these efficiently or consult the handbooks. Libraries often have training CDs or videos about how to use the well-known brands available for borrowing. Applications might be easier to use if they resemble paper products that we are used to. Other applications should be investigated and used if they increase productivity. To save time we can:

- print out pages from our computer organiser only when we require them to save carrying a large paper organiser
- set up our organiser to automatically record regular dates and move forward ongoing commitments
- send database, spreadsheet or word processing documents to colleagues online

Email

Emails make corresponding quicker and cheaper. But some managers can receive up to 200 emails every day. If we spend all day answering our emails we will not have time to do any other work. Most of the time wasted by emails is caused by sending unnecessary correspondence. Our friends and colleagues do not need a copy of the latest round robin email joke nor attachments of photos of the office party. We must resist the temptation to copy emails to everyone in our address book or send long personal messages. There are some simple way to reduce the time taken to answer emails.

1 Delete unwanted emails.
It is usually easy to spot the junk (spam) emails by their subject headings. Delete them unread.

2 Answer emails at set times.
Decide to answer emails twice a day, perhaps once in the morning and once in the afternoon. Do not read emails between times.

3 Prioritise emails.
Answer important emails immediately and leave the rest until a convenient later time.

4 Use standard replies.
Prepare standard replies to common questions and paste these into emails when appropriate.

5 Deflecting emails.
Ask staff to copy emails to other people only if they require action from those people.

Email etiquette:

- Don't write or pass on unsuitable or irrelevant emails
- Don't write in CAPITALS – it's like shouting
- Keep emails short and succinct
- Put the main point of the email in the subject line
- Don't send personal emails from work

Voicemail

Many office computers can accept and send voicemail. This can save time but only if you set up your voicemail efficiently. Make sure that the message the callers hear is up-to-date and relevant. Listen to voicemail twice a day and reply to important messages as soon as possible. As voicemail is sometimes turned off during working hours we must check that voicemail is on when we leave the office and arrange for it to be transferred to our mobile if we are out of the office during the day.

Viruses

Computer viruses can destroy a computer's entire hard disk and all the programs and work that are on it. It is easy to install and use a virus checker. The company technical department should help. Once it is installed use it regularly – once a week is the absolute minimum. Never download unknown programs from another computer or disk nor allow staff to do so. If a new program is necessary the company technical staff should be consulted. The time taken to do a regular virus check is small compared to the hours or days that would be lost if a virus attacked your computer.

Tips on saving work:

- Save work at frequent intervals throughout the day
- Download work regularly on to removable disks, preferably at the end of each day
- Make a back-up copy of start-up disks and programs
- Keep dated back-up copies of work in a safe place

Tomorrow we look at how to keep phone calls under control.

Taming the telephone

Today we are going to look at ways of taming the telephone. First of all we will look at telephone mismanagement and the traits of the telephone junkie. We will then look at techniques for controlling our incoming calls and for making our outgoing calls more productive.

Taming the telephone

- The telephone trap
- The telephone junkie
- Incoming calls
- Outgoing calls

The telephone trap

Many of us make and receive dozens of calls every day of our working lives. The telephone is an invaluable management tool. It allows us to communicate instantly with people anywhere in the world. It is more cost-effective than travelling to a meeting and quicker than written communications. There is a downside, however, in that we are instantly accessible to anyone who wishes to speak to us regardless of how unimportant the issue or inconvenient the time. Our use of mobile phones has also made us more accessible and encourages us to chat. We can say 'no' to a meeting and throw a low pay-off letter in the bin but as soon as we pick up the telephone and hear, 'Let me tell you about our new photocopier', 'About the letter I sent you', or 'I just rang to see how things are going', we are trapped. Someone else is determining how we spend our time.

The secret of good telephone management lies in eliminating, or cutting short, the junk calls while getting the most from the important ones.

The telephone junkie

Telephone junkies have a detrimental effect on everyone in the office: too many unnecessary calls are made, too much time is spent on each call, important calls are not returned, items agreed upon during calls are not followed up... the list is endless. We all exhibit the traits of the telephone junkie from time to time. The following questionnaire will help us to determine how often.

Telephone junkie questionnaire

Do I:

	Sometimes	Always	Never
rush to answer the phone as soon as it rings?	☐	☐	☐
spend longer on calls than is really necessary?	☐	☐	☐
have to make calls twice because there was something I forgot to say?	☐	☐	☐
allow telephone calls to interrupt my meetings?	☐	☐	☐
dial numbers and then forget who I called?	☐	☐	☐
drop what I'm doing when I remember a call I need to make?	☐	☐	☐
not screen my calls even when there is someone available to do so?	☐	☐	☐
spend more than 30 seconds dealing with unsolicited sales callers?	☐	☐	☐
finish calls without covering the topics I want to discuss?	☐	☐	☐
scatter my outgoing calls randomly throughout the day?	☐	☐	☐
write down messages on the handiest piece of paper at the time?	☐	☐	☐
forget to pass telephone messages on to others?	☐	☐	☐

Scoring the questionnaire:
For each 'sometimes' answer, we should score ourselves 1 point; for each 'always' answer, 3 points, and 0 points for each 'never' answer. A score of 16 or more puts us into the telephone junkie category and we need to sit back and evaluate how we are using the telephone. Why are we not

URGENT!

using it productively? What needs to change before we can gain control over the telephone? Even a score of less than 16 means that the telephone probably rules our lives from time to time. The questionnaire will have helped in identifying those areas we specifically need to work on today and in the future. We should use our score as a benchmark to gauge our improvement over the coming weeks and months.

Incoming calls

The telephone rings continuously during the day. A certain proportion of our incoming calls bring good news or provide useful information, while the remainder are unnecessary. Unfortunately we cannot tell before picking up the phone which calls are important. Managing incoming calls is therefore partly a damage limitation exercise. We need to keep the unwanted calls brief, and the important calls productive.

We should not give our phone number to everybody because that increases unwanted calls. We also need to be aware of the security problems of using phones in public places. Private business information may be overheard or a mobile phone could be stolen together with any private contacts saved on it.

Most of us underestimate the length of time we spend on the phone during the day. Setting up a telephone log, as shown below, will therefore be a revealing exercise. Every call we receive today should be noted along with its duration and pay-off. Our time management notebook should be used for this exercise.

Telephone log: incoming calls

Date:

Time	From	Re:	Duration	Pay-off
9.20	sales	photocopier	5 mins	low
9.50	S. West	set up sales meeting	17 mins	med
10.30	D. Martin	in meeting, asked to call back	2 mins	low
11.00	M. George	query on memo	11 mins	low
11.20	client	sales order	13 mins	high
11.48	sales	training course	4 mins	low
:	:	:	:	:
:	:	:	:	:
4.50	A. Smith	tennis game	15 mins	low

Total time spent on incoming calls: 2 hrs 5 mins

Looking back at our telephone log at the end of the day we will undoubtedly be shocked at the number of calls we have received and their duration. We should set aside five minutes to analyse our calls and ask ourselves the following questions:

- How many unexpected calls did I receive?
- How many unwanted calls did I receive?
- How many calls lasted longer than necessary?
- How many calls could have been dealt with by someone else?
- How many calls interrupted me when I was busy with a high pay-off item?
- How many calls could have been screened out?

It pays to practise techniques for keeping our junk calls brief. In our time management notebook, we should note down at least three excuses we can use, such as, 'I'm in the middle of a meeting right now can you tell me very quickly what you want', 'I have a taxi waiting for me', or 'I have a conference call booked in about two minutes'.

I'LL HAVE TO HURRY YOU – THE BUILDING'S ON FIRE AND THE FLAMES ARE LICKING AT MY DESK...

When the telephone interrupts our work, many of us have a tendency to scribble notes on the nearest piece of paper, whether it is a letter or an open report. This habit creates problems for us when we need to go back and find someone's telephone number or check on the price we quoted. Which bit of paper were we using at the time? Where did it go? For important colleagues or contacts, we should set up an index card or a page in our personal organiser. Each time they ring, we can turn to their page and immediately see what the last conversation was about or if there are any items we need to discuss with them. The key points of the current conversation can be captured and retrieved quickly if we need to refer to them.

The checklist below outlines 10 important techniques for managing incoming calls. We should try to use them all throughout the day. If we have problems with any of the techniques we should develop strategies for overcoming them.

Techniques for managing incoming calls

- Put phone on divert or DND when busy
- Set aside a quiet hour during which we will not take calls
- Ask for all calls to be put on hold during meetings
- Be polite, firm and brief with unwanted sales callers
- Ask people to call at particular times when we are less busy
- Avoid tackling peripheral tasks while on the phone
- Avoid taking notes on loose bits of paper
- Arrange for calls to be screened whenever possible
- Ask the receptionist not to give out names to cold callers
- Make a list of excuses for keeping calls short

Outgoing calls

Outgoing calls are more manageable. We can decide who we wish to speak to, when we make the call, what we want to say, and we also have greater control over its duration. A telephone log should be set up for outgoing calls in our time management notebook.

Telephone log: outgoing calls

Date:

Time	To	Re:	Duration	Pay-off
10.20	Personnel	job advert	8 mins	med
12.00	Personnel	forgot to ask about salary details	3 mins	low
:	:	:	:	:
:	:	:	:	:
3.20	J. Coates	arrange meeting	24 mins	med

Total time spent on outgoing calls: 1 hr 38 mins

Towards the end of the day, when our outgoing calls telephone log has been completed, we should ask ourselves the following questions for each call:

- Was the telephone the best way of getting the message across?
- Did I achieve my objective?
- Did I waste too much time on small-talk?
- Did the call drift into low pay-off areas?
- Did the call last longer than anticipated?
- Was there anything I forgot to say?

Planning the call

Most outgoing calls are made on the spur of the moment.
We are sitting at the desk and we suddenly remember we
have to call someone. We pick up the phone without
thinking and launch into the call. As a result we forget
things we want to say, we put things across badly, and we
fail to get the information we need.

Before making any call we should ask ourselves: what
information do I need to pass on? What information do I
need to obtain? What is the best way to get the message
across? What papers do I need to have to hand for the call?

Making the call

We should treat each call as a mini-meeting. We should
ensure that we get our own message across, and that we
capture the other person's ideas. It is a good idea to
summarise quickly the points made during the call, to make
sure there is no confusion. We should block off time in our
diary once or twice a day and make our outgoing calls
together. Grouping our calls will motivate us to be brief and
to the point. Our calls should also be prioritised and then
made in order of priority. We should also create a sense of
urgency with our lower pay-off calls by setting a definite
time limit.

After the call

Any action points that arise as a result of our discussions
should be followed up immediately or written down on a
to-do list.

The checklist below provides guidelines which should be
followed for each outgoing call made. We should block off

time in our diary for tomorrow and make a list of all the calls we need to make.

Checklist for managing outgoing calls

- Plan calls as if attending a meeting
- Make outgoing calls in blocks
- Prioritise calls
- Set limits on the duration of each call
- Collect relevant documents before the call
- Summarise discussions before the end of the call

Mobiles phones

The time management techniques in this chapter also apply to mobile phones. But although mobile phones can save us time by enabling us to keep in contact with the office, they can also be great time wasters. Just because we can get football results or listen to music on our mobile phones does not mean we should. Nor do we need to spend time sending and receiving text messages from our friends. We should switch our phone off during meetings and use its voicemail facility so that we can decide when to respond. We should not use our mobile phones for personal calls during office hours.

Most people reading this chapter at work will have been constantly interrupted by unnecessary telephone calls. The techniques in this chapter should help to reduce this problem and make the telephone a more productive management tool.

Tomorrow, we will look at managing meetings.

Managing meetings

Most managers spend somewhere between 30 and 50% of their working lives in meetings: drop-in visitors, committee meetings, recruitment interviews, brainstorming sessions, crisis meetings and conferences. We all know that an unacceptable proportion of the time spent in meetings is wasted.

Today, therefore, we are going to explore ways of maximising that time investment. First of all we will try to identify some of the factors behind unproductive meetings. Then, starting afresh, we will look at what should be done before, during and after our meetings, whether as chairperson or attendee, to make them more productive. We will examine checklists that can be followed for all meetings, whether they are one-to-one discussions or more formal gatherings.

Managing meetings

- Why do meetings go wrong?
- What to do before meetings
- What to do during meetings
- What to do after meetings

As a means of communicating, meetings can prove very useful. They enable us to:

- Transfer information and receive feedback
- Generate new ideas
- Build consensus for a decision or course of action
- Combine expertise to solve problems

Things can go wrong, however, as hinted at in the business adage, 'In all your parks and all your cities you'll find no statues of committees'.

Why do meetings go wrong?

We should set aside about 20 minutes to evaluate our current meeting management skills. The first question we need to ask ourselves is, 'What proportion of my time is spent in meetings?'. Next, we should ask ourselves, 'What proportion of that time is wasted?'. Thinking back over the meetings we have attended in the past few weeks we should explore the following areas:

- How much did the meetings cost?
- Were the costs of attending the meetings greater than the benefits gained?
- Were the meetings adequately planned?
- How many meetings were delayed because of late-comers ?
- Did the meetings frequently last longer than expected?
- Were there problems with equipment and facilities?
- Did I make worthwhile contributions to the meetings?
- Did other participants make worthwhile contributions?
- Did the meetings tend to wander away from the agenda?
- Were decisions, taken during the meeting, followed up?

Now that we have identified the potential pitfalls, we will turn our attention to making our meetings more productive. We will start with the meeting preparations.

What to do before the meeting as chairperson

Whether guiding a formal meeting or arranging an informal chat, it is our responsibility to make sure that the right people are in the right place at the right time and have received the relevant background information. The checklist below should be followed before each meeting that we organise. Preparation is the key to success!

Chairperson's checklist

- Is the meeting really necessary?
- What are the alternatives to meeting face to face?
- What are the objectives of the meeting?
- Who is needed to ensure that these objectives are achieved?
- What will be the pay-off from achieving the objectives?
- What will the meeting cost?
- What equipment/facilities are needed for the meeting?
- If an agenda is required has it been prepared/ distributed?
- Are all the attendees clear about the start time and location of the meeting?
- Have attendees received all the relevant background information?
- Do all the participants need to be present for the whole meeting?

At first, we may find working through the checklist a bit laborious, especially for smaller meetings, but over time, the questions will become ingrained in our memory. Running through the questions mentally will become a matter of habit and as a result our meetings will become more productive.

What are the alternatives to a meeting?

How many of the meetings we attended in the past week could have been replaced by a brief chat, a memo, a quick telephone call, a decision by the person in charge? Could the issues have been added to the agenda of another meeting? Before arranging any meeting we should look at all the other alternatives.

The meeting's purpose

We should clearly define the the meeting's objectives, and communicate them to participants when arranging the meeting. This gives others the chance to prepare in advance and ensures that people do not have to sit through an irrelevant meeting because they thought it was going to be about something else.

The meeting pay-off

Once we have set the objectives for the meeting, we need to ask what the pay-off from achieving each objective will be. The pay-offs will enable us to prioritise the agenda and focus on the important items. The total meeting pay-off should be weighed against the meeting cost to see if it is a worthwhile exercise.

NICE AGENDA !

Preparing the agenda

As the number of participants in a meeting increases, so the
need for an agenda grows. The agenda should be kept brief
and uncluttered. The agenda items should be positive and
achievement oriented, i.e. 'To find a solution to the
distribution problem', rather than 'To discuss distribution
problems'. The highest pay-off items should be placed at the
top of the agenda so that if we run out of time, the major
issues will have been covered.

What to do before the meeting as attendee

As meeting participants, we need to evaluate the necessity
of attending the meeting and to be well prepared. There is
nothing more infuriating than sitting through a meeting
which, with the benefit of hindsight, we know we should
not have attended. We should learn to guard the precious
asset, our time, more carefully. Instead of attending, we can
save time by talking to people who have attended or by
looking at the minutes afterwards.

What to do during the meeting as chairperson

As chairperson, we need to be aware of the destructive forces that can make meetings unproductive. We will look at some of the more common forces, along with strategies for coping with them.

Late-comers

We should never reward the late-comers and punish the punctual participants by holding meetings back until everyone is present. If we are lax about start times, we give participants licence to make extra phone calls or to chat with colleagues in the corridor before the meeting. We should, without exception, start our meetings on time. As soon as the meeting starts, the door should be closed. As late-comers

arrive, we should never interrupt the meeting to bring them up to date on what has been discussed.

Hidden agendas

At the start of the meeting, attendees should be asked what they personally want to get out of the meeting. We will then get the hidden issues and concerns out into the open where they can be addressed. Participants hi-jacking the meeting to promote their own agendas should always be interrupted and reminded of the true purpose of the meeting.

Rambling discussions

The only way to stop long-winded or irrelevant contributions is to interrupt. We should wait for someone to take a breath, jump in, briefly summarise the point being made, and move on.

Low participation

We should actively try to encourage the participation of attendees by reacting positively to contributions. There is no quicker way to silence a group than to be over critical. If someone with potentially useful contributions is silent, we should ask them directly for their ideas. Asking people to confer in pairs or smaller groups is another useful technique for getting things started.

Interruptions

There is a famous story about a US senator in a meeting with the President. The phone was ringing continuously and the President was getting involved in a protracted conversation each time he picked it up. Eventually, the senator left the room and called the oval office extension. He immediately got the President's attention.

We should arrange for all calls to be put on hold for the duration of our meetings. 'Do not disturb' signs should also be used for office doors indicating the time that the meeting will be over. If someone does break through our initial barriers, we should arrange a time when we can get back to them.

Arguments

If people are arguing unproductively during meetings, we should suggest that their discussions be continued outside the meeting. If that is not possible, we should acknowledge the differing points of view and ask participants to focus on a solution. In larger meetings, we can bring arguments to an end by asking for a show of hands on the issue.

Group indecisiveness

There is no point having meetings where lots of things are discussed but nothing is decided. After each item on the agenda has been discussed, we need to summarise the decision taken, any follow-up actions and deadlines. If

possible, we should produce an instant action summary
during the meeting and distribute photocopies to
participants as they leave.

Decision/action to be taken	Person responsible	Deadline
Letter to be sent	J.D.	12/5
Report on product launch	G.H.	22/5
Sales conference details	J.D.	22/5
New computer system	M.G.	28/5

On paper, many of the suggestions for controlling meetings
look straightforward. In the middle of a meeting however,
they will appear a lot more difficult, and the easiest option is
to do nothing. We need to practise these techniques, meeting
after meeting, until we get them right. A start can be made
by analysing the effectiveness of our next five meetings and
making a checklist of areas in which improvement is
needed. If we learn how to control destructive forces, our
meetings will be dynamic, productive and enjoyable.

Chairperson's checklist

- Always start on time
- Set out the objectives for the meeting
- Stay positive throughout the meeting
- Follow up actions from the last meeting
- Decide who will take the minutes
- Encourage participation from reserved attendees
- Silence sidetrackers
- Keep the discussion focused on the agenda
- Adhere strictly to the agenda timetable
- Summarise decisions/actions to be taken as the meeting progresses, and again at the end
- Ensure that all the items on the agenda are covered
- Finish the meeting on time.

What to do during meetings as attendee

As participants at meetings, we should always try to be constructive. If we act counterproductively, we are wasting our own time as well as that of the other participants.

Attendee's checklist

- Contribute constructively to the meeting
- Restrict contributions to agenda items
- Focus on the meeting's objectives
- Be clear about any follow-up steps to take
- Avoid private discussions during the meeting

What to do after meetings as chairperson

What happens after the meeting, ultimately determines whether or not the meeting has been a success.

As soon as the meeting is over the chairperson should quickly work through the questions below. In certain circumstances it can be useful to evaluate the meeting with the participants.

Chairperson's checklist

- Has the meeting been a success?
- Were the right participants present?
- Were all the items on the agenda covered?
- How should unfinished items be dealt with?
- Do I need to distribute meeting minutes?
- What should I do differently next time?
- Could we have achieved the same results without a meeting?

What to do after meetings as attendee

The meeting we have just attended is worthless unless actions are taken as a result of the discussions. After the meeting has finished, we should transfer any follow-up actions into our to-do list and ask ourselves the questions below.

Attendee's checklist

- Was my participation in the meeting really necessary?
- Am I clear about any follow-up actions I need to take?
- Did I contribute constructively to the meeting?
- What should I do differently next time?

Holding virtual meetings

Now that business is conducted nationwide and worldwide it
is not always possible for individuals to attend all the
meetings they need to because of the time and cost of travel.
Virtual meetings are therefore becoming more commonplace.
Meetings can be held by video link, telephone or on the web.

What happens at a virtual meeting?
The link is set up beforehand and booked with the supplier
if necessary. The meeting takes place at a prearranged time
and the participants in each place assemble beforehand in a
special room. At the arranged time the link is opened and
participants can communicate by phone or video link even
though they are not in the same place.

Rules for a successful virtual meeting:

- Ensure everybody is assembled on time
- Arrange for a secretary or colleague to refuse entry
  to anyone once the meeting has started
- Make sure everyone is seated where they can
  head, see and be heard
- Allow for a time delay

Meetings can be a productive way of getting things done but
they can also be an unnecessary drain on our time. If we pay
attention to getting things right, the rewards throughout our
careers will be enormous.

Tomorrow, we shall take a look at project management.

Managing projects

Today, we are going to look at fine-tuning our project management skills. There are three stages in managing a project: planning, controlling and evaluating. If we fail to manage these three stages effectively, the project may well end up in the project graveyard. A quick glance through the papers on the desk or gathering dust in the filing system will invariably reveal many projects which we started enthusiastically but which were never completed.

> *Project management*
>
> • Planning
> • Control
> • Evaluation and review

A project is a series of interrelated tasks leading to a definite end. We spend a large proportion of our time juggling projects ranging from writing a report to launching a new product. Smaller projects can be dealt with by writing the individual tasks on our daily to-do lists, while larger projects require a more sophisticated approach. It is these larger projects on which we will concentrate today.

Working through this chapter provides us with the ideal opportunity to plan a project which we are about to take on. After reading the chapter once, we should choose a project and work through it according to the principles outlined. We should also compile a list of all upcoming projects in our time management notebook, and schedule time for planning them properly.

Before going on to look at the three stages of project management, it will benefit us to look at the 10 most common reasons why projects fail.

1 Taking on too much
2 Inadequate planning
3 Project costs outweighing benefits
4 Ineffective delegation of project tasks
5 Procrastination
6 Failure to spot potential problems
7 Focus on more immediate, but lower pay-off, items
8 Lack of overview
9 Lack of a clearly defined objective
10 Poor communication between members of project team

Looking back over the last three unsuccessful projects we took on, we should compile a list of the reasons why they failed. Once that has been completed, we can look at ways of ensuring the success of our future projects.

Planning

The more time we spend planning the project, the easier its
implementation will be. With project management, we need
to be pro-active rather than re-active. We need to anticipate
problems rather than waste time trying to sort them out
once they have occurred.

There are five major stages in planning a project. Each stage
should be followed as we plan a current project.

1   Identify the objective
The objective provides the focus for all the individual tasks
that must be performed as part of the project. It should be
stated clearly and concisely because, if the objective is stated
ambiguously, then the different members of the project team
may end up working towards different ends. The questions
below will help us to identify the objective. A project
overview page should be set up in our time management
notebook for each project we undertake and the answers to
these questions written down.

- When the project has been completed I will have achieved . . .?
- What problems will the project help to solve?
- How will the project be completed?
- Who else will be involved in completing the project?
- What is the scope of the project?
- How long will it take to complete the project?

2 Cost-benefit analysis

Many projects are undertaken without proper consideration of the costs involved and then when these costs escalate alarmingly during the project, it has to be abandoned. For the project we are currently planning, we need to examine the costs of undertaking it, as well as the rewards to be gained from completing it. These rewards may be financial in terms of increased revenue or decreased costs. The intangible rewards which cannot be measured in financial terms should also be considered.

- What tangible benefits will result from the project?
- What intangible benefits will result from the project?
- What are the costs involved in completing the project?
- Do the benefits outweigh the costs?

In our time management notebook, we should compile a list of costs on one side of the page and a list of benefits on the other. The project should only proceed when we are satisfied that the benefits outweigh the costs.

3   Break the project down into individual tasks
Sometimes, when we are faced with a large project it can
seem overwhelming. Where do we make a start? Often, we
make a start, but not at the beginning, and then leave key
tasks until it is too late and we have a crisis on our hands.
On one page in our time management notebook, we should
break down the project into its individual tasks. Start with
the major tasks and break them down into smaller tasks
until everything that needs to be done has been identified.

For each individual task, we need to ask, 'What could
possibly go wrong?'. The answer to this question will help
us to set up contingency plans.

4   Schedule the tasks
Alongside each individual task we should write down an
estimate of how long it will take to complete. Next we
should decide on an appropriate deadline for each task.
Many tasks can be completed at the same time, while others
may have to be performed sequentially. We should be
realistic here and allow for delays. It might take us 10
minutes to obtain an item of information from a colleague,
but it may take us a week to arrange a meeting with them.
Once we have completed our scheduling, we can set a
deadline for the project. Finally, the deadlines should be
transferred to our to-do lists for the relevant day. Key
project tasks which, if not completed will cause the project
to fail, should be highlighted on our to-do lists.

5   Delegate tasks where appropriate
Many of the projects we undertake will involve us working
with others. This means that the project workload will be

spread out, and we will also benefit from the input of others at the planning stage. When delegating tasks, we should negotiate a deadline for their completion and write it down on the relevant to-do list.

Delegation is the art of getting things done through others. As we progress through our careers, we will find it necessary to rely more and more on our colleagues to get things done for us. Many managers fear delegation and the loss of control it brings, but it is essential to free up our own time for higher pay-off activities.

Five steps to effective delegation

1 Communicate clearly what needs to be done
2 Agree a deadline for completion of the task
3 Let go of the task and trust the delegatee
4 Reward successful completion of the task
5 Be considerate and avoid dumping tasks on others

We should spend five minutes writing down all the activities that should be delegated to others.

Recording a project

Keeping an accurate record of a project is vital to its success. By recording the stages as they are planned and due to be carried out, a check can be kept on how the project is progressing. At the end of the project the record will show which strategies were successful and suggest ways in which the next project could be improved.

Keeping basic records

Project records do not need to be complicated but they should be made regularly and kept up-to-date. If possible, keep them in one bound book or loose leaf folder. The records should include:

1 The project's aim, participants, expected timescale and cost.
2 A plan of the project including a day by day plan.
3 Details of who will be doing what and by when and confirmation of when each action was completed.
4 A running account of costs.
5 Notes of problems and possible solutions.
6 A daily, weekly and monthly summary of results.

The project manager should keep the overall record but individuals should keep their own records so that these can be checked with the main record. In large projects there will be particular record keeping roles for an accountant.

Control

Project control is the process of monitoring projects to ensure they are on track, and taking corrective action where necessary.

The project overview in our time management notebooks will prove invaluable during this stage. When we are dealing with a large number of projects, essential tasks may slip through the cracks. We should constantly refer back to our list of tasks on our project overview page and tick them off as they are completed. If there is a lot of time-sensitive paperwork involved in the project, we will need to use a bring-forward system for keeping track of everything.

One or more project files should be set up and kept in an accessible place. We should purge the file after each major stage of the project has been completed, so that we are not constantly shuffling through piles of unnecessary paper whilst looking for something important. Many people leave all their project paperwork on the desk and say, 'I have people coming into the office all the time to discuss things, so I need to have everything where I can lay my hands on it'. However, this method means that important documents often get buried, and the papers relating to different projects get scattered around and mixed up.

The most important part of project control is to avoid being distracted by the urgent but unimportant items that land on the desk every day. We can easily fall into the trap of getting busy with the quick, easy, fun and comfortable paperwork while the important things hibernate at the bottom of the in-tray. Using a prioritised to-do list, we should constantly monitor ourselves to ensure that we are focused on the high pay-off project tasks.

Control checklist

- Monitor scheduled project tasks on a daily basis
- Always assign an 'A' priority to project tasks
- Keep track of delegation deadlines using the diary
- Periodically refer back to the project overview page
- Use a bring-forward file for time-sensitive paperwork
- Keep project paperwork together in a project file

Evaluation and review

Reviewing completed projects is a brief but essential exercise. During the planning stage, the evaluation should be scheduled as the final project task and this will help us to avoid focusing on activity rather than achievement. If the project has not gone according to plan, the review enables us to analyse what went wrong so that we can avoid similar problems in the future. If the project has been successful, the review enables us to identify why things went well, to acknowledge the positive contribution of others, and to congratulate ourselves. Any lessons we learn during the completion of a project should be noted down on a special page in our time-management notebook. This page can then be reviewed during the planning stage of future projects.

When evaluating the project, we should ask ourselves the following questions:

Project review checklist

- Was the project objective achieved?
- Was the project completed by the deadline?
- If not, why not?
- Was adequate time assigned to planning?
- Were all the project tasks identified beforehand?
- What avoidable crises occurred during the project?
- What problems could have been avoided by prior action?
- Were the right people involved in the project?
- Was everyone motivated to complete the project?
- Was the project completed within the allocated budget?
- What would we do differently if we could start again?

Finally, we should rate the overall success of the project on a scale of 1-10.

We are now equipped with the right tools for tackling any future projects. Our professional reputation in the long term is dependent upon our ability to manage projects effectively.